MythBusters
Lessons from Active Black Fathers

By: Marvin A. Banks

MythBusters: Lessons from Active Black Fathers
Copyright © 2020 Marvin A. Banks

Cover design by: Savage Graphix Bar
ISBN: 978-1-7360697-0-7
Library of Congress Control Number: 2020921806

All rights reserved. No part of this publication may be produced, stored in a retrieval system, or transmitted in any form or by any means-electronic, mechanical, photocopying, recording, or otherwise- without prior written permission of the publisher or copyright owners.

Published by Robinson Anderson Publishing, LLC
15922 Eldorado Parkway
Suite 500
Frisco, TX. 75035
www.rapublishingco.com

Dedication

To Puggy and Ditty...I hope that I have made you proud.

To Dee Dee, Titi, KeKe, Mimi, and Jay...you all gave me a reason to live. All I do is for you.

To Greg, Brandon, and the entire 4th floor crew. Thank you for inspiring and motivating me daily with your actions.

Table of Contents

Dedication	iii
Prologue	vii
Chapter 1: Marvin, Senior: The Dad's Dad	1
Chapter 2: Sparky: The Loving Father	13
Chapter 3: James: The All-Star Dad	23
Chapter 4: Travis: The Community's Dad	33
Chapter 5: Value Your Seed	41
Chapter 6: The Village	49
Chapter 7: Evolving as a Father	55

Prologue

MythBusters: Lessons from Active Black Fathers

"If I were to fail as a man, a husband, or a father, that would dishonor my father's legacy, and I have no desire ever to do that."

There is a myth in America that black fathers are absent from black children's lives. "In 1965, then-New York Sen. Patrick Moynihan published "The Negro Family: The Case for National Action." It argued that the number of women-led households in black communities was the largest obstacle to black people achieving economic and political equality. Since then, the issue of "missing black fathers" has been a top priority for black intellectuals, activists and community leaders, as well as a favored retort from people seeking to deflect from conversations about structural racism." Admittedly, 57 percent of black children live in households without their bio logical fathers, while 20 percent of white children experience the same reality. Yet, this statistic doesn't tell the full story. From the time of slavery, when men were forcibly sold away from their families (or their families were sold away from them), and for generations after that, uncles, grandpas, cousins, coaches, and family friends have filled the critical space reserved for fathers. Thankfully, in the black community, the absence of a biological father need not deprive a child of the opportunity to have a "Dad," whether naturally born to them or not.

Additionally, many black men take an active role in raising their children, even if they are not present in the home. Gone are the days of the traditional nuclear father home by five smoking a pipe by the fireplace while reading the evening newspaper and waiting to hand out advice to his doting children. Today, there are late nights, FaceTime calls, and strategically placed text messages to fill that void. Furthermore, resourceful black women continue to rely on father-figures who thrive in the role and provide the structure, encouragement, love, and support their children need to become fully functioning, thriving adults.

Being a black man in America creates unique challenges that take a mental, physical, and emotional toll and make being a good father even more difficult. Yet, despite this challenge, so many men surpass "good" and manage to be great fathers to their children, providing the emotional, financial, and moral support their children need to flourish. They make it look easy, but it's anything but.

I am writing this book as a tool for fathers with lessons and guidance from myself and some of the best black fathers I've ever met - each of whom is strong, uplifting, disciplined, and driven by character, responsibility, and dedication. These men are never afraid to show love to their children, those they fathered biologically, and those they "stood in the gap for." Why would a man take on the responsibility of children that are not his own? Love. Those men who raise and nurture children who are not their own often do so because they have a relationship with the children's mother that inspires them to protect, love, and provide for her children, who, in turn, become their children. I know this firsthand because I am a father of four despite not being the biological father to any of my four children. My wife and children are the biggest blessings in my life, and I can honestly say they all helped make me the man I am today.

Fathers are needed, fathers are necessary, but most of all, fathers are human. They are subject to the same trials and tribulations as mothers but often bear them quietly. Among these challenges is the struggle to maintain healthy relationships with their children's mother and the children themselves as they grow and mature. Fathers often must step outside of themselves and sacrifice for their children's emotional and financial needs in ways they never imagined that they would want to. This alone creates stress as fathers seek to increase their earning potential and income to provide for any and everything that their children might need. Fathers must also set their natural pride and hubris aside as they seek to help their children navigate the difficulties they will inevitably face in school or sports. Despite the adversity facing them, some fathers rise to the challenge and meet that adversity with a sense of perseverance and pride that dominates every other emotion and characteristic. I know many such men, and I hope to use their knowledge to inspire others who may be just starting their fatherhood journeys and feel uncertain or challenged in ways they never imagined. If you're such a father, you need to know that those fathers before you went through some of the same things and can offer some incredible guidance if you simply seek out their knowledge. You have taken the first step by reading this book, and I humbly offer these pages as a glimpse into the insights I've gleaned from the incredible Dads I know.

It is important to note that this book will not tell you how to raise the "perfect" child. It will not tell you how to produce a college-bound D-1 athlete, a Rhodes scholar, or the next black president. Instead, this book offers examples to guide men down the path of great fatherhood

- the most important job any man will ever have. My hope and prayer is that this resource will provide useful guidance for fathers who aim to be better Dads through leading by example, loving unconditionally, supporting emphatically, and growing in maturity to meet the challenge of being a great father head-on.

1

Marvin, Senior: The Dad's Dad

Long before I became a Dad, my father shaped not just the man I would become but also the father I was destined to be. I learned the ways of fatherhood by watching his example. Marvin Sr. shaped every aspect of my character as a man with the way he carried himself, his integrity, and his intellect. In the words of Mahatma Gandhi, "Manliness consists not in bluff, bravado or loneliness. It consists in daring to do the right thing and facing the consequences...It consists in deeds, not words." Studying my Dad as he navigated life helped me when I reached uncertain waters.

At 6'3", my Dad was a giant of a man who loved everyone. He was a man's man - tall, handsome, incredibly smart, fiercely protective of his wife, my mother, and dependable. Armed with a great personality and an infectious laugh, he was always the life of the party and could make even the most hardened soul laugh along with him. In high school, some of my girlfriends would comment on how fine my Dad was, much to my dismay. Even though I was mildly embarrassed, I still felt a sense of pride (and hoped that his suave sophistication passed on to me).

Marvin, Sr. spread life and love everywhere he went - an essential trait for any great man - because it is inner joy that makes a man strong in the face of adversity. As I reflect on his life, this trait continues to marvel me. Despite his status as a hero in my book, I knew he was an ordinary person who had faults and problems like the rest of us, but who somehow never let life's disappointments take away from the love and joy he shared with his family. He loved everyone, especially his nieces and nephews, whom he treated like his own children. Without even knowing it, my father, Marvin Sr., was preparing me for the most challenging yet rewarding blessing I'd ever have with his example of unconditional love - that of fatherhood.

His Work

Dad was brilliant. Had he not been born black in the 1930s during the era of Jim Crow and segregation in Knob Noster, Missouri, I believe he would have had the opportunity to pursue an education, maybe even become a doctor, which was his dream. Instead, my father enlisted first in the Army, where he served as a medic during the Korean War. He was later discharged from the Army and enlisted in the Air Force. Dad often talked about how disappointed he was that he could not take advantage of the benefits offered to white veterans to pursue college. Like many black veterans, the higher education and homeownership dreams that catapulted white families to wealth did not become a reality for him. He felt as if his training on the battlefield prepared him for a career in medicine, but sadly, the doors to higher education were closed. His hopes were dashed when his first job out of the military was a nursing assistant position at the Veterans Administration Hospital. Although it was an honorable job, this position often called for challenging tasks such as changing diapers for incontinent patients. Additionally, the pay was low, so he took a job at Goodyear and remained there until he retired, never fulfilling his dream, despite his brilliance.

For some men, this setback would have been devastating. All too many black fathers in the same position allowed themselves to become consumed with despair and emotionally separated from their families and friends. Not so for Dad. Even though Marvin, Sr. didn't fulfill his professional dreams, he was still full of happiness. He had a brilliant sense of humor and a knack for making the right joke at the right time. He had a goofy laugh that was infectious and would last an eternity, it seemed. That kind of joy comes from deep inside.

His Family

Like many black men then and now, Dad revered his mother and treated her like a queen. They always had a close, loving relationship, and she spent every holiday with us when I was young. As she got older and experienced medical issues or her home needed repairs, my father would drop everything and drive two hours and go to be with her to ensure that he took care of her. When she could no longer live alone, my grandmother came to live with us. He taught me through his actions that mothers were to be cared for and respected always.

Marvin, Sr. had two brothers, Uncle Junior and Uncle Lonnie. Uncle Junior, the oldest, had two children, and Uncle Lonnie, the youngest, had seven children. All of my paternal first cousins are older than me, so my Dad had plenty of children to spoil and love on before my siblings and I came into his life. He was the quintessential "favorite uncle" who treated his nieces and nephews like his own, giving them gifts for birthdays and holidays and always providing love and support.

Because of his charm, welcoming personality, and great sense of humor, he was the favorite uncle. As a child, he was given the nickname Puggy, but his nieces and nephews called him "Uncle Pug." When my Dad met my Mama, and his attention shifted to her, he still kept the favorite uncle's title because of his consistency and presence in his nieces and nephews' lives. Dad had been married twice previously, but he had no children when he met my mother. Looking back on it, I think Dad probably thought he couldn't have children. That is until my mother became pregnant with me.

My mother, who was affectionately known to her family as "Ditty," was strong, college-educated, intelligent, and fiercely pro-black long before it was ever fashionable. Mama had been married previously as well and had three sons whom she worked hard to support. Mama was a firm believer in self-reliance. The Civil Rights Movement was incredibly important to her, and she would often watch videotapes of black civil rights leaders. She often told me that had she grown up in New York, Chicago, or Oakland she would have been a Black Panther.

My mother was the darkest and only brown-skinned woman of her siblings and was abused and mistreated because of it. For this reason, she detested colorism. I can remember growing up, the one sure-fire thing you could do in our house to get your ass kicked was making a dark-skinned, light-skinned joke. Whenever this happened, my mother unleashed her wrath on the offender. She didn't play about this, and everyone knew it. She instilled in me a sense of black pride that clearly defines me to this day. My mother was my best friend.

My Dad spent many years as a second father to his nieces and nephews and had a wealth of experience spoiling children and giving them the things they needed to be successful and happy. However, there were other aspects to fatherhood he was just beginning to develop. Providing comfort and an attentive ear to his children's problems did not come naturally to him. Despite that, he often gave my brothers and me sage wisdom in the form of witty quips about being a man that always made us laugh. Those quips stuck with me, and I still apply them to this day. As I mentioned before, my Dad had an incredible sense of humor, but there were times when he was serious in his delivery of the knowledge he chose to impart.

One bit of guidance my father often gave to my brothers, and I was this, "If you love the woman, you got to love the child." While some may cringe at the grammar in that sentence, it does not make the spirit of the statement any less powerful. My father meant that if you love a woman and she comes with children, you also have to love those children like they are your own -not as your stepchildren - your own. They are your children, and you must treat them that way. My father lived by those words his entire life. More importantly, he instilled them in me, and his guidance shaped me for my role as a father years before I assumed that responsibility.

My father stepped into his role as a father to four sons without trepidation simply because he loved my Mom. When Mama told Dad that one of us needed something, his response was always the same, "Don't worry about it, we got it." Was my Dad really able to provide everything we needed? Truthfully, the answer is no. But on the rare instance he couldn't, he still managed to impart wisdom. He taught us to have pride and not to beg others for help. He often said, "If I can't get it for you, you don't need it." I share that sentiment with my family to this day.

My brothers were much older than I, so they were practically out of the house when I came along. Dad had a good relationship with them for the most part. Growing up, I watched some of my friends endure the treatment of stepfathers who, more often than not, disregarded or even mistreated them while all of the attention and affection went to the biological children of the stepdad. It always struck me as odd because my father never treated my brothers in that fashion. My father was the opposite of those fathers, and my older brothers called him "Pops," a sign of the respect and affection they had for them.

Because my brothers were "grown and gone" when I started school, my mother no longer had to split her time between three children and was able to give me her full attention. My Dad, ever the provider and the encourager, told my mother when I was very young that her only job was to ensure I got an education. Dad was determined that I would not fall victim to the systemic racism which prevented him from reaching his dreams and was equally determined that I would get a good education. When I reached a point where my mother could no longer teach me at home, my Dad paid for tutors and any other educational help I needed to ensure that I achieved what he did not.

Like my father, my mother was very driven. She grew up in Topeka, KS, the epicenter of the Brown vs. Board of Education legal battle. She saw first-hand the effects of systemic racism. She saw the black community work together when it had no choice before desegregation. She yearned to see our community come together and work cooperatively again. My father made it his mission for me to be college-educated so that I could overcome the obstacles he faced as a young man. On the other hand, my mother knew that to fight racism, a black man needed to be twice as smart and twice as good. She was determined that I would be both. While the objective for their missions was slightly different, the goal was the same. Me failing at becoming a learned man was not an option.

My father was very protective of my mother, but his protection also extended to his children, nieces, and nephews. If you were in need, he was the person that you could call because you knew he would come to the rescue no matter the situation. He was going to answer, and he would be by your side to help you through. Because my father was so protective, my grandmother tagged along on all our family vacations to babysit us because my Dad only trusted her to watch me while he and my mother went to spend time alone. By this time, my older brothers lived on their own, so Dad spent more time with me. He taught me how a man should take care of, honor, and revere his mother. I wish my son could have seen me do that for my mother so that he could learn by example as I did.

My father's legacy is the memory of what he instilled in me and in how I move through the world as a man. His values inspired me to graduate from college, pursue my MBA, and become the man and father I am today. I took his values with me to college. After I graduated, I traveled to Mexico and lived in Kansas City before eventually moving to Houston, Texas to start my career (and use the Spanish language I'd spent years becoming fluent in). It was a friend who encouraged me to move to Houston because of the substantial employment opportunities and affordable quality of life there. I was a bachelor at the time who grew up in Topeka, Kansas, and I was interested in playing the field in a new metro area and experiencing all that the dating scene had for me.

Of course, I met the love of my life and the woman who would become my wife the second week after I moved to the city.

When a Man Loves a Woman

It was 2004, and I was a new man in a new city. I'd been out a couple of times in the city and liked its vibe. It more than met my expectations in terms of social scene and nightlife. For the first two weeks, at least. After I met "her", I was off the market for good.

Stephanie was tall, beautiful, cocoa brown, and had the most beautiful smile I'd ever seen and a laugh that was just as infectious as my father's. I loved everything about her, including how her voice sounded, her style and grace, and, most importantly, her tenacity. She was tough, and even as a young woman, she had her life together. When I was sleeping on my air mattress in a one-bedroom apartment, Stephanie had a fully furnished, beautifully decorated apartment that was comfortable and cozy. She was working full-time, going to school full-time, and was a fully functioning adult. Most importantly, she was one of the strongest, most caring people I'd ever met.

When I met her, she was 25, and I was 27. She told me from the start that she had a two-year-old son. She asked me if her having a child was a deal-breaker. Of course, I said no, but I hadn't really thought about dating a woman with a child before. It wasn't that I was resistant to the idea; it was just that the opportunity hadn't presented itself before.

When we started dating, and the relationship became serious, I knew that I'd eventually meet her son. I admit looking back, that I was a little nervous about meeting him because my father's words rang in my ears.

"If you love a woman, you got to love the child." I wondered more than once if her son would like me and if the bond between us would grow as effortlessly and as strongly as it had between his mother and me. It seems funny to be intimidated at the prospect of meeting a two-year-old and consciously thinking about being accepted by a child that young, but I can tell you that is a real fear for any man who has been in that position.

When the time came to meet her son, Darnell, I knew immediately that I would grow to love this child like my own. Like most little kids, he was all smiles, and when we met, he came to me and threw his arms around my legs in a hug. At that moment, I think I physically felt the weight of the anxiousness I had about meeting him melt away and I just felt at ease.

I thought about how much I loved his mother already. How we just clicked from the beginning. She was confident and strong, and I saw what a wonderful mother she was to her son, and I knew that not only would she become my wife, but we would become a family. That her son would become our son and that I would embody my father's words of wisdom on fatherhood.

From the moment I met Darnell, I treated him like my son. He had a father; however, he wasn't very involved. When I got a haircut, I took him to the barbershop with me. When he needed to see a doctor or the dentist, I took him when she couldn't take him. In every respect, he was my son from the moment I met him, and since he's been a presence in my life since the age of 2, he doesn't remember a time when I wasn't there for him. We were always together.

Besides having a two-year-old, Stephanie soon began to help her mother raise three little girls who were her biological cousins. She played a huge role in caring for not only her son but the three little girls she and her mother agreed to raise. Over time, my role in their lives, along with Stephanie's, increased, and we became parental figures for the girls. My girls (as I affectionately refer to them) lived with us off and on through their formative years, and when they did not live with us, they spent time at our home almost every weekend. Family vacations and trips almost always included them. I was their father figure, and they eventually began to refer to me as Dad, a title I gladly accepted.

A few years after my wife and I got married, I received a new job, and we eventually moved to Omaha, Nebraska. We did not want to leave Houston. We had a multitude of friends, classmates, and family nearby. Plus, who would want to leave Houston, Texas, a city with a multitude of things to do, to move to Omaha, Nebraska? But alas, the opportunity for a career change was too good to pass up, so we packed up and left. At my behest, I extended an invitation to Stephanie's mother and the girls to come with us. Those were my girls, and I couldn't stand the thought of leaving them behind. Many people criticized me for this decision. But their opinions mattered not. I had made an internal commitment to be the father those girls needed, and any mockery or second-guessing that may have come from someone else was insignificant to me.

When we moved to Nebraska, it was always a shock to people when they learned that Darnell wasn't my biological son and, when they realized it was true, most people didn't believe it. I legally adopted him when he was ten years old, and he asked to take my last name. It was one of the proudest moments of my life, but even if I'd never adopted him legally, in my heart, he would have always been my son. The adoption was essential to me and to us as a family, so we made it official.

I got a lot of recognition for stepping up to the plate to be a father to my children, but I didn't do it for that reason. I have always told people that whatever kind of blessing I was to my wife and children, it paled in comparison to the gift they gave me by allowing me to be a part of their lives. They have taught me patience, unconditional love, and were much more of a blessing to me than I ever expected.

Often, I'd get compliments, such as "I admire what you're doing," or "you're such a good man." I looked at my role in their lives much differently. They didn't ask for me to come into their lives, I came into their lives, and I told them that I would be the father they needed. There were also people in my life that considered me a fool for taking on four kids who weren't biologically mine. A few times, I heard jokes about being a play dad or not a real dad. I found that I could fend off those attacks with a quick response or a glaring stare, but it did play into my own insecurities, if I am honest.

As a young father, I often feared that my children may one day challenge me or disrespect me because I wasn't their biological father. It was a source of a lot of insecurity for me, especially leading up to the rebellious teenage years. I constantly worried that they would say things like, "you aren't my real Dad," and I knew I'd be crushed. It's hard to pour into a child all that love and devotion and watch it evaporate under the weight of teenage petulance, and I knew it would devastate me.

My insecurities weighed so heavily on me that I had to discuss my feelings with one of my mentors, "Sparky." I knew he was just the right person to have this conversation with, and I never regretted sharing this with him. His response is what eventually set my mind at ease in my role as father. Our talk put my insecurities to rest. Thankfully, by the Grace of God, I never heard those words from either of my children.

Questions for Discussion

1. What did your father's example (good or bad) teach you about manhood and fatherhood? Do you want to be like your dad or the opposite of him?
2. What examples are you setting now for the children in your life that they will remember and imitate?
3. Why are the children of the woman you love to be treated like your own children? Can you think of examples in history or culturally where this was or is standard practice?

2

Sparky: The Loving Father

Every man should have that "go to" dude who is like a big brother that they can ask anything. Ideally, this is the guy who would give you the guidance you desperately need before you need it, and then, right when you are about to make the biggest mistake of your life, you remember his words. That guy for me was Sparky.

Sparky and I first met after I was initiated into my fraternity. He was like a brother and was among the first friendships I made with an older brother while in college. He was a husky former football player with a loud, gruff voice that carried across a field. Contrary to his gruff exterior, Sparky had a gentle laugh, which could make anyone smile. Although he had a nice side to him, he was actually fearless and always seemed to be around to keep the young brothers on the straight and narrow. I wasn't always a fan of having an older brother around to keep an eye on me and keep me from doing things I probably shouldn't do, but there he was.

Although he was about 10 years older than us, Sparky always hung around whenever we were having an event. It was often annoying because he was so much like a big brother, so I would intentionally hide from him and not answer his phone calls, so I could keep doing whatever foolishness I was up to without having to answer to anybody.

I did this on several occasions, and then one day, Sparky caught up with me. He was on to me. He looked me dead in the eyes and said, "Look, man, you are mine; when I call you, you answer the phone." I never ducked one of his calls again.

Sparky was that dude who would tell you openly and honestly that he loved you without the slightest bit of machismo or awkwardness, and you knew he meant it. He told me that often, especially when I needed to hear it most during some of the most challenging times of my life.

It wasn't so much that Sparky was a choir boy - he wasn't - but he was the kind of dude who could see a little bit further down the line than most men who were about to make a silly, callous, or life-altering mistake. His guidance came from experience, as he himself had made mistakes and would tell you that. This is what motivated him. His mission was to keep you from following in his footsteps. There's a saying that goes, "a hard head makes a soft behind." Sparky doled out the advice that would prevent you from getting the soft behind, and he did it because he usually knew he was speaking with a hard-headed individual, which was definitely me as a twenty-something.

Sparky taught me many life lessons. Though he smoked cigars and frequently drank Crown Royal, he told me not to drink too much, especially when in public. He lectured about giving back and being of service. It's not that it hadn't occurred to me, but I hadn't quite decided how I wanted to give back. He talked to me about assisting him with the sports league he founded coaching boys basketball. One day, he called me and said, "Practice is today and Thursday. I'll see you at the school."

When I showed up at the school that Sparky had instructed me to arrive at, there were 15 young boys in front of me and no Sparky. I had no idea what to do, so I fell back on the days when I played basketball. I tried to coach them through some drills, and it was a complete mess. Eventually, Sparky showed up and took command. He barked out orders, and the children followed through without hesitation. It wasn't the first time Sparky had taught me about being a man and a leader through example, but it definitely is one I will never forget.

In addition to coaching, he also helped kids with life skills and finding a vocation if they didn't like school. He had a way with even the most challenging kids. The fact that they respected Sparky and listened to him had less to do with his physical size or his deep voice than most people would have thought. He had a significant impact on the young people he coached and mentored, and they gave him the highest respect in part because in him they had a man who would listen to them without judgment, offer tough love, a tender hug, and treat them with respect. Even the most disagreeable teenager would listen to him because of his presence.

I think he felt a personal mission to help other young people navigate the tough years by providing the lessons and guidance he wished he'd had so that they could avoid making mistakes that would deprive them of the future they deserved. Besides being a teacher by profession, coach, and a fraternity brother, Sparky had a family. He had two small daughters who were seven and nine, and he was very much a presence in their lives, although he was no longer in a relationship with their mother. His girls adored him, and it was easy to tell that he loved them as well.

Sparky taught me about the importance of fighting for your family. He married right after college and had two daughters, but the relationship didn't work out, and they divorced, but he got custody of his daughters and raised them as a single Dad, which was and still is very unusual. His ex-wife lived in another city a couple of hours away.

All of us brothers got to witness Sparky raising the girls, and from him, we learned a lot of lessons on what it meant to be a dad (it takes work). He didn't have the best relationship with the mother of his daughters, and he said there were times when having a civil conversation with her was difficult, but he worked hard to maintain a positive relationship with her for his daughters' sake. He would always say that you don't let any obstacle come between you and your children.

I remember once Sparky called me and asked me to go on a road trip with him and his two daughters because he was taking the girls to visit their mother for the summer. He mentioned on the drive that he wanted me along for company and as a witness because he felt that his ex-wife would try to keep the girls. Ultimately, that's exactly what happened. Many men would have given up at that point and just said, "it is what it is," but that wasn't Sparky. He was determined to fight his ex-wife in court to regain physical custody of the girls.

About a year later, Sparky told me one of our fraternity brothers saw his daughters at a step show they were putting on for their elementary school. He told Sparky how one of his daughters came to him and said," Do you know my Daddy? And called Sparky by his line name." Sparky told me that when he heard this story, he broke down crying. He missed his daughters terribly, and he was committed to getting them back.

As a teacher and coach, Sparky didn't make a lot of money, but what he had, he exhausted fighting his ex-wife to regain custody of his girls. They were the most important thing to him in the world, and he wouldn't have been able to deal with it if anything happened to them because he wasn't with them to watch over them. He was a protective father and a proud man who understood the importance of fathers in their children's lives.

When Sparky regained custody of his girls, he was happy again. It changed him for the better, and you could tell that a weight had been lifted from his shoulders. Eventually, he met a lady who became the mother of his third daughter. He wasn't in a committed relationship with her at the time, but that did not stop him from taking responsibility for and being a presence in his daughter's life. He was there for her just as he was there for the first two, and though he didn't have custody of his third daughter, Sparky would drive 2 hours to see her whenever he could. When his third daughter's mother got married, he respected his daughter's relationship with her stepfather, but he set the example as her father and made sure that his daughter always knew that.

Sparky had many positive characteristics, but like everyone else, he wasn't a perfect person. He made mistakes, but he never tried to hide them or deny responsibility for them. That is what made him so different from many men I knew because he had this sense of personal responsibility that was admirable. He eventually met another lady and settled into a live-in relationship with her and had a son. The two of them seemed to have a great relationship, and Sparky was overjoyed to have someone new to spoil and shower attention on and soon settled into the life of a middle-aged Dad, teacher, and coach.

Whenever I talked to Sparky, he was happy. It wasn't that he didn't have problems; he had plenty of those. But he was content to be doing what he loved – teaching, coaching, and being a Dad. Whatever his faults may have been as a person, he excelled in his role as a coach, mentor, and father and held himself accountable for the mistakes he made elsewhere. He wasn't the kind of man who would stay down when confronted with life's hard knocks but would get up, tend to his wounds, and charge back out there to try again.

He had the opportunity to move beyond the high school level and coach at the collegiate level because he excelled in his job. He declined the opportunity because he had to stay involved with his kids. Moving was not an option. It was much more important for him to sacrifice that job to remain engaged in his children's lives.

Sparky and I remained close over the years, and when I started my own family, we'd often have conversations about being a father. In those early years, I was very insecure about raising another man's child, and though I loved my son, I didn't know if I wanted to fully invest my heart and soul into nurturing a child who might one day say the most cruel words that a child could utter to a father, "you're not my Dad."

The thought of hearing those words haunted me in those early years a lot more than I care to admit. My insecurities about those words were rooted in the fact that I had heard friends and family speak to them in anger or frustration when the "stepparent" dared to deliver anything close to parental guidance. From the kid's perspective, you were encroaching on territory that didn't belong to you, and generally, once those words were said, you knew the kid wanted you to butt out. I was petrified that after all of the love, nurturing, and support, I gave my children they would one day say those words to me, and I would be mortally wounded as a parent. I never heard those words. Not once. And I never had issues with my son's biological father, but the thought of hearing them kept me in fear for the first few years of fatherhood.

I confessed to Sparky one day about my fear of hearing those words. I was seriously contemplating proposing to my wife. My insecurities about stepping up full-time to raise her son were bothering me tremendously. We had that straight talk relationship where I could tell him things like that without the fear of being judged or being thought of as too soft. With Sparky, I could be completely vulnerable. We were just men talking about one of man's biggest challenges: navigating fatherhood. I desperately needed his advice and knew he would understand where I was coming from.

Sparky listened carefully as I told him my fears. When I said the words I dreaded most, I followed those words with a question to my friend, "How do I respond to that?"

Without missing a beat, Sparky looked at me and said, "You tell him you were the father he needed when he needed one." It was the most straightforward advice, but I'd honestly never thought about how I would respond if I ever heard those horrible words or just how painful it would be to hear them. Sparky made sure that I was prepared with a response, although I'm grateful to this day that I never needed it.

As I said, Sparky liked to live and was a ferocious partier during his free time. He smoked cigars, drank, was at least forty pounds overweight, and had a high-stress job teaching and coaching. Most men, he didn't take his health nearly as seriously as he should have and rarely saw a doctor.

When he was just 49, Sparky died of a massive heart attack. His death was among the most painful I've endured in my adult life because we were so close. He was my confidante, my big brother, and my friend, whose talks I miss daily and whose shoes will never be filled.

Because he was such a beloved member of the community and so loved by the thousands of young people whose lives he touched, his funeral service housed an overflow crowd. It was clear from the many tributes that he had a profound impact on people during the short time that he lived. Sparky would have been happy to hear such beautiful words spoken about him.

As I reflect on my friendship with Sparky, I can only be grateful for the many lessons he taught me through his lectures, his example, and his service. Many people assume that a person who is successful in certain areas of their lives has an immunity to problems in other areas. Nothing could be further from the truth. What set Sparky apart was that he was accountable to himself and shared his most difficult lessons and tips for avoiding making the same mistakes he had made along the way. Sometimes, he did that by telling a funny story or a joke but always with a sense of humility and relatability. You couldn't help but take him seriously, even if he made a critical point by telling a joke because he would eventually get to the part where he'd tell you that he messed up, and that it cost him something important, and that he wanted you to avoid making the same mistakes.

Sparky taught us about service and being a good influence on young black men's lives. The message was that it was a blessing to have the ability to go to college and have an impact on young black boys at an early age. That was what service looked like, and it wasn't optional.

Through his works of service, his legacy still lives on. He founded a basketball league that still exists. There was a scholarship established in his name, and people donate every year to ensure that two students from the high school that he coached go to college. His influence inspired me to make sure that I influenced my children even when they didn't make the best choices.

I honestly can't think of a man who had a more significant influence on my life than Sparky, including my Dad. My father was a great provider, but he didn't know a lot about being a motivator and encourager. Dad didn't know about being present, being open, or being vulnerable. I learned all those things from Sparky.

Although Sparky was a tough guy, he was also man enough to be comfortable displaying his emotions, and I would learn over the years spent with him that it was ok to display your emotions as a man. The thing that I appreciated about our bond was that he was never afraid to tell me that he loved me. When he died, it hurt me tremendously because I lost that mentor and guiding light and haven't been able to replace it.

I had no way of knowing back then how useful Sparky's counsel would become to me as a father. It wasn't just that he taught troubled kids how to get on the right path; he also helped young men like myself identify what real manhood, and eventually fatherhood, looked like - it was leading by example, encouraging without bullying, and showing up when you say you will. We all knew he wasn't perfect, but everyone respected him. Above all, we knew that Sparky would hold himself accountable for his failures. This is a lesson that I have taught my son: to be man enough to own up to your mistakes. When you do this, you may still suffer the consequences of the mistake, but you face it like a man.

A man can show strength and still allow room for vulnerability and emotion. Being a strong man and a leader doesn't mean you can't also be gentle and loving when needed. Sparky taught me that there was time to be tough, but that should be followed by love. That advice has served me well as a father. Sparky chose to be of service using sports to get and keep young people active, engaged, and out of trouble. Sports would play a big factor for me as a father as well. Being involved in sports is how I met James.

Questions for Discussion

1. What can you learn from Sparky as a father and mentor? What can you learn from his story about self-care even as you are caring for others?
2. Are most men comfortable displaying their emotions in front of others or saying, "I love you?" How does this impact their relationships?
3. Why is it important to share your mistakes and successes with children (either your own or those you are mentoring)?

3

James: The All-Star Dad

Most Dad's introduce sports to their sons and daughters at an early age as a way to bond with their children, give them structure, and keep them active. If you're lucky as a parent, your kids will naturally gravitate toward one sport, fall in love with it and begin to hone and practice their skills to become better and better at their game.

I believe that most Dads secretly harbor a fantasy that their sons will make it to the NBA or NFL, which is part of the reason that involved Dads are so diligent about keeping their sons involved in sports. As a young father, that was me.

Being involved in sports is something I wanted for Darnell early on, and he had his first opportunity to participate in football when he was about 6. Though I was adamant that he participates in sports, my son was a little man at about the same time that there was a big controversy surrounding whether or not young boys should even be playing contact sports like football. I was somewhat resistant to the idea of Darnell playing football for that reason. At the time, the head injuries some boys received while playing football were all over the news. At the same time, pro athletes, doctors, and scientists also expressed concern about traumatic brain injuries caused by repeated concussions. There was also a lot of concern that the risks were substantial and that parents should re-evaluate sports. Eventually, we determined as parents that the level of concern wasn't high, and the benefits of being involved in sports for kids far outweighed the slight chance of physical injury, so our son would play. This was fortunate for me because enrolling my son in football was how I met James.

One day, my wife and son were at the park when an older man saw my son and thought he would be a good fit for his football organization. I was still hesitant about him playing tackle football, but I begrudgingly went along. To say that my son was enthused about playing football would be an understatement. He was tenacious and showed no fear when it came to hitting. At the time, my son was about 7, and he showed early prowess in football, and I was happy about that, even if I had my concerns about him playing at that age.

Several coaches were dads as well. They each had a son playing on the team. One of them was a big guy with a voice that carried like Sparky's. His name was James. James was a couple of years younger than me at 30 and was an engineer by trade. You could tell that he was a serious guy, but he also had a friendly personality, was funny, and laughed often. He didn't take himself too seriously, even for a competitive guy. We talked for a bit and hit it off. I found out that he also had two young sons who played for our football organization, the Cy Fair Ravens. James also had a wife who was pregnant with a third son.

I noticed early on that the Ravens coaches and Dads were very involved in the sport with their boys and that they were good men with only the best intentions and goals for their kids and the rest of the team. That immediately made me want to be part of the team and to be around these guys who I thought were setting great examples for the boys and involved in a way that demonstrated that they wanted to inspire greatness in their kids.

As a coach for the Ravens, James was a big guy with a voice that carried the distance of a football field. We were both big guys, but James was the one with the louder voice. I often watched him do his thing with the players. I also noticed that while he was firm in coaching the kids, he also built them up after giving them the criticism that they often deserved when it came to making mistakes.

James had a nickname for each one of the kids and a certain way of getting them to listen even if he wasn't particularly sensitive in his delivery. He genuinely cared about the kids, however, and because of that, the boys always wanted to make sure that he was proud of them as a coach.

After one incredibly tough game with a rival team, James gave a speech that was very moving and inspirational to the boys. It was so moving that I called him to thank him for it afterward, and our bond as brothers began to build.

As football ended, basketball season was just around the corner. We discussed transitioning our boys to basketball, as his son, Darnell, and my son, Darnell (our sons shared the same name), were both going to need an indoor sport to play. There was no organized basketball team, so we decided to form one, which we comically named the "Houston Heavies" since we were both big dudes.

We recruited kids I coached at the YMCA, and he brought some boys from the neighborhood to form the team that turned into a miniature AAU basketball team. It was rough, and there were a lot of practices and games that weren't pretty. But we were Dads who not only wanted to give our sons an opportunity to participate in the sport but also mentor and develop focused and dedicated young men. I was head coach, and James was assistant, but it was clear from the start that I was in over my head. It wasn't that coaching in and of itself was difficult because I'd done that before, but I had never coached my son before. Up until that point, I only had one role, and that was Dad.

The thing about my son was that even at 7, he was a phenomenal athlete. He was fast for his size and had incredible instincts that would help him to make plays that would leave people in awe. But he was also young, talkative, and like all kids, sometimes didn't follow directions well. Although he was a great athlete, it was a challenge to coach him, and I didn't want the other parents on the team to think that I was playing favorites by having him out there on the court so much. I didn't want the other parents to accuse me of playing what we called "Daddy Ball," where you put your kid in because you think he's great while neglecting another boy who was equally or even more talented. I wanted to avoid that at all costs.

Though my son played a lot, I was very hard on him. I'd yell at him and be sharp with him. In every practice, I wore the coach's hat, and it didn't come off when the practice was over but would often last well into the evening after we got home. Every day, my son had to deal with the coach in practice, the coach after practice, and then the coach in the evening. Rarely during basketball season did he have the opportunity just to enjoy being with his Dad.

There was one time that was really stressful because we were playing against a team that was highly skilled. We had the boys doing layups warming up for the game. I wanted the boys to focus on boxing out for rebounds, so they were running to get into the proper position. They were supposed to box me out for practice. My son was not paying attention and ran right into the side of my knee at one point and it caught me off guard. It also hurt, so much that I grabbed him roughly and said, "Get your act together!"

When I returned from the main court to the sidelines, I went on about my business coaching the game but noticed that my phone was buzzing off the hook. I went on to try to coach the game, but my phone kept buzzing. Thinking it was an emergency, I looked at the text messages. It was my wife, who was sitting in the stands. She was letting me know that I was being too rough on our son and that I needed to chill all the way out.

I hadn't thought about the way that I sounded to my son, but clearly, my wife had witnessed it and thought I'd gotten too upset over the whole thing. It made me reflect on the times that I'd yelled at my son in the past and how he would often be quiet, not talking as much after practices and games and just shutting down. It never occurred to me that he could have been emotionally upset with my aggressiveness and mistake that for anger. I realized that I was putting undue stress on our relationship by not putting a delineation between coach and Dad. My competitive nature and my desire to see him do his best was what drove me to demand a certain level of performance from him at all times, but I didn't know how to scale that back or keep it in the proper perspective.

Then one day, I had a conversation with James, who had been facing the same challenge with his oldest son, who was also on our team. We talked about the importance of being competitive but without breaking the kids' spirits with our drive and aggressive coaching style. We agreed then that it had become a problem that we had to address.

We came up with a brilliant solution: we'd swap kids when it came to coaching advice. James would coach my son, and I would coach his. This gave each boy a chance to get guidance from a coach with a similar mindset while not enduring being with "coach" rather than Dad all the time. It was so simple; we were both kind of shocked that we hadn't thought about it earlier.

The change in the boys was immediate and helped forge a bond between James and me. We understood one another. We were both fiercely competitive and had the determination to instill that drive in our boys and be the kind of Dad that they could respect and appreciate off the court or field.

There's a very fine line between motivating your child and crushing their spirits. Fathers (and even some mothers) are often so fiercely determined or competitive that they cross that line. It's tough to witness as another Dad does this, but if we're honest with ourselves, we'll admit that we've exhibited some of the same humiliating behavior, though that was not our intent. We need to do better.

As a team, we took a lot of defeats, but we built bonds within the community. Our organization impacted those young men's lives, and for that, we're both grateful. In addition to having a positive impact on the team, I earned the respect and friendship of another father who wanted the same as I did for my son: to motivate him to always give his best shot, play hard, be determined to win, and to be fair. I also learned over time that James was very similar to me. Not just in his approach to coaching and motivating young people, but also in his seriousness about his role as a husband and head of his family. While he could be a tough coach, he was also very loving toward his sons and his wife. I learned from him that I didn't have to be this hard-driving, no-nonsense tough guy all the time, and it was important to show love as well as inspiration as a Dad and husband. Also, when you give that tough coaching guidance, follow that with love so that you're not destroying a person's spirit.

James really taught me that being a Dad is trial by error. One thing that I respected about him then and now is that he was always willing to learn. He took coaching and being a Dad very seriously, and he read books and would subscribe to different newsletters on how to be a great father, husband, and coach. As an engineer, his mind was analytical and logical, so the intellectual in him naturally sought those kinds of resources. No, a book can't teach you everything you need to know about any of those roles, but it can help spur you to see where you might be making mistakes and how to correct your own deficiencies or actions in order to become a better husband or Dad.

As men, we are told that we are the head of the house at a very young age. That's something that my Dad certainly taught me, and as I said, it was his role as a provider that was the most influential teaching he instilled in me. Men are also protectors, and with those roles, there comes a level of authority. Our roles as men should be handled with strength, but also some level of sensitivity. As James and I discussed these issues man-to-man, it became clear that although James was younger than me by a few years, I could learn a thing or two from him.

Setting my ego aside, the more we talked, the more I began to think about how my approach might need to change in my role as a husband and a father. I began to think about the type of father and husband I was versus the kind of husband and father I wanted to be. Did I fall short? Was I too quick to get angry or upset about things? Was my guidance or criticism also tempered with love and encouragement? As I considered these things, I realized that I wasn't perfect. But who is? That said, I needed to make some adjustments. James was the person who helped me see that maybe I could be better at both roles, and I didn't mind at all that he was a younger dude imparting that wisdom when I needed it.

The great part of my friendship with James was that we were tight, but our families were also close. Though James and I initially vibed because we had sons the same age who even had the same name, we would later find out that we enjoyed many of the same things, so it was easy for our two families to hang out and bond. I respected James because he was smart and resourceful, and I liked to hang out with him because I gravitate toward people I can learn from. We both wanted our sons to be successful basketball players, and we were each passionate about that.

We also did the same kinds of things as a Dad for our kids. I'd leave work to buy my son the latest sports games or shoes, and I would find James in the same sporting goods store buying his son the same things. It was comical that we would wind up at the same place at the same time so often. When my family moved from Houston to Omaha, and I had to leave the area, and the team, James, and I remained closed. Our sons remained friends, and the basketball organization that we started continued to be successful.

It's good to look back at that time, more than ten years ago, and realize the progress that I made both as a husband and a father since then. James looked for opportunities to learn how to be better in every role he played – husband, father, coach, and he often sought that knowledge from books. I later realized that he also sought it through developing connections with other like-minded men who saw their roles as fathers as among the most important activities they would ever undertake and prioritized continuous improvement in those roles. There was a lot to admire in James' approach to leading and evolving over time and also how to respond under pressure.

At his core, James was a calm person who would gather the facts and not be too quick to respond with an emotional reaction. I can't say that I was the same back then. No, I wasn't abusive, verbally or physically, but I often didn't temper my response with love, and I see many men making the same mistake.

I learned that it was just as important to show love as encouraging athleticism, good sportsmanship, and a competitive nature. Whether we realize it or not, our children are always watching our behavior, looking and learning from us and not all of their knowledge comes from verbal interactions. Sometimes, facial expressions and non-verbal cues convey negative emotions that we might not even realize we're displaying. These things also induce a stressful reaction in the body, and none of that is good physically or emotionally. So, we have to be better about releasing that anger and tempering our negative emotions with more positive words and actions. We can still love and appreciate sports and competition, but family comes first.

James and I have had a great friendship and have enjoyed many activities where we bonded with other men who had sons involved in competitive sports. The connections I've made through my involvement with my son in sports have been too many to count, but many of them were made through my initial friendship with James. As we left Houston to start a new life in Omaha, I would meet several other dads who would have a positive impact on me as a man. One, in particular, was named Travis.

Questions for Discussion

1. What dreams do you have for your children? Do you push them to be the best at what they do? Is this positive or negative?
2. What can you learn from James about how to be a "competitive dad?" How can you motivate your children without crushing their spirits?
3. Do you believe it is possible to coach and father a child at the same time? What does this look like when this is happening in a healthy way?

4

Travis: The Community's Dad

A consistent theme throughout my journey with fatherhood is how essential sports have been in cementing my relationship with my son early on and meeting other dads who were as serious about the job as I was. As he continued to mature and his athletic ability increased, sports became much more prominent in our lives. It also became the primary means by which I connected with likeminded men who wanted to be active with their sons while encouraging them to put in the work to become better at their game.

After I relocated my family from Houston to Omaha for work and enrolled the kids in school, my next priority was finding a basketball team for my son. Regardless of where we moved, that was always a priority. My son was the type of child who needed to be involved in some activity to burn his energy. And I found that through sports, making friends in a new city would be a lot easier. Another advantage that came with it is that it also became the means for me to meet new people and other fathers who were actively involved with their sons in pursuing the sport of their interest.

When my son Darnell and I started to research basketball teams that he could play for, we eventually settled on the Omaha Warriors. I'd first heard about the team from one of my fraternity brothers. There was one standout athlete on that team, and his father was Travis, who was the father of two sons. After signing up for the team and attending Darnell's first practices, I met more of the parents and eventually developed friendships with this engaged network of Dads, who all had boys who played sports. They were also typically very involved in the community. Some of their involvement centered on social groups like their fraternities or church organizations, so many of us had that common bond in addition to sports.

Though Travis and I pledged different fraternities, which we joked about often, he welcomed us with open arms into the Warriors basketball team and to Omaha. Travis was a high-level administrator with the local public-school system, was well known, and had a lot of influence locally in the community and among most of the black parents in the city. His impact on the community was widely known, especially in the areas that would benefit the most from civic involvement, which was one of the things that I admired about him the most. We hit it off immediately and formed a tight-knit friendship.

Though Travis was a few years older than me, we had similar temperaments. We'd both get overly excited or agitated from time-to-time during the practices and games, and we would take turns calming one another down. There were times that he would be livid about something that happened during one of the games, as parents tend to do, and I'd have to calm him down. Other times, I'd be close to throwing a punch at one of the game officials or the parents, and he would have to walk me to the side and have a private conversation with me about why that wasn't the best idea. I think everyone needs a guy like Travis in their lives.

Even though I learned many lessons about fatherhood from James, I still struggled to parent a young boy and teach him not to be weak or cower from life's challenges. I called Darnell my little soldier. From the first day I met him, he was a pretty tough kid who could handle almost anything. He was extremely competitive. When we lost a game, it was not out of the ordinary for some of the children to cry about the loss. I would never allow Darnell to do that. I would tell him that he better not shed a tear about a game. At the time, he was about 8, so old enough to listen, but still a very young child. Like most young children, complex emotions hadn't quite developed, so in response to anger, frustration, disappointment, and many other things, his immediate reaction was to cry. It's almost instinctive.

As a man raising a son, the last thing you want to see is your son crying. Darnell's team would lose a game, and he'd naturally be disappointed. You could see it all over his face, which registered hurt, anger, sadness, and shock all within seconds while he fought hard not to cry. All I had to do was give him one look, and he would soldier up. He knew that's what I expected, and he responded as I had taught him to. Eventually, even he began to look at other players who cried over a loss as weak.

I don't recall the exact moment it occurred to me that telling my son that he better not cry over a game might have been counterproductive. I'd been doing it for so long without thinking that it was harmful, but slowly, I began to see that I was teaching him to suppress his emotions. Almost every man I know has told his son not to cry when they are upset. Most men believe that somehow crying makes a boy weak, but I know that's not true. Slowly, it dawned on me that teaching him to suppress his emotions and telling him not to cry might be detrimental to him mentally and emotionally.

Men and boys experience the same emotions as women and girls and should be allowed to cry when they want. One mistake we make as men raising sons (or just being around other men) is that we're quick to advise one another to suppress our emotions and get over it and move on without fully dealing with or expressing our emotions. Travis taught me a lot about that.

Travis was probably the poster child for emotional intelligence, a fairly common psychology term used today but which few people talked about years ago. It means being aware of, in control of, and expressing one's emotions in a judicious and empathetic way. He was a compassionate dude who would console and encourage someone to express an emotion in whatever way they felt comfortable while not criticizing how they chose to express that emotion.

Travis knew I expected Darnell to be a tough guy all the time and would encourage him to "man up" when he even thought about being what I considered to be weak. Travis told me to allow my son to process his emotions in the way that he chose to process them. He reminded me that although our sons were big for their age and top athletes, they were still babies.

My conversations with Travis helped me see that I didn't allow my son to process his emotions. Travis always put those things into perspective with me. He used to say things like, "Marv, don't sweat the little stuff." If Darnell did something that was wrong or silly, he would ask if it was something that warranted a response or not. He'd ask me to consider if it was something that was intentional or if it was an accident. Could the problem be avoided the next time or was there a bigger lesson in it either for Darnell or me? That was honestly something I'd not thought a lot about before that stage.

When you're the father of a son, you try to instill values and knowledge into your child that will serve them as they grow and mature. The one thing that you may not realize as a father, though, is that most men have historically been taught to suppress their emotions, and this can be very unhealthy for boys. Without being allowed to express emotions, men grow up bottling anger, frustration, and disappointment in a way that impacts them emotionally, educationally, or psychologically. Suppressing emotions is particularly damaging to kids, especially boys, whose minds are still developing.

We deliver the message that crying or expressing emotions is something only girls do when in reality, everyone does it, and it's perfectly healthy. Allowing boys to vent their frustration is healthy and normal, but often in our effort to make them tough, we impede their ability to process things emotionally. Some men don't even want to talk to their sons about how they feel emotionally after a setback or disappointment. Marvin Senior was a perfect example of this. As men, we have to learn to talk with our boys and listen to them as they express the range of feelings they have to give them guidance on how to move forward after they've vented their frustration or other emotion.

Darnell was a kid who was a great athlete and was good at football and basketball. He was naturally gifted. Yet, he was still a kid who would sometimes show a lot of immaturity and do things that would impede his progress. That's when I spent the most time developing lines of communication between the two of us. One of the smartest moves I've made as a Dad is establishing a relationship with my son where he felt comfortable enough to talk to me about the things that were happening to him on a day-to-day basis without fear that I won't listen or will judge him first. It definitely was not always like this.

Applying Travis's mantra of "don't' sweat the little stuff" helped me build the relationship that I wanted with my son. It also made me think back to when my father had given me grace after I had done something in defiance. When I was 14, I got my ear pierced, something I knew would make my mother angry. As expected, she went ballistic when I got home from the mall and showed her the piercing. She was as mad as I'd ever seen her, and I was more than a little afraid that she would never get over it. My Dad had to calm her down by reminding her that I was a good kid, hadn't been in any trouble, and if the worst thing I had done was gotten my ear pierced that they had to be doing something right. He helped her see that a pierced ear wasn't as bad as she thought, and I wasn't on the fast track to the state penitentiary. I was just being a teenager. Travis' mantra made me think back to that story and readjust my approach with my son.

Travis and I were outlets for one another. We often would talk about our sons, the pride they brought us, and the silly or stupid things that they had done that defied everything we taught them. Any situation that involved my son where I knew I would be too emotional to respond constructively; I would ask Travis about and get his opinion as to whether I was overreacting. I would often ask how he would handle it, and he always had the right words, the right demeanor, and the right approach that would help me find a smoother approach or an answer that would address the problem.

Travis also established a rapport with my son. He didn't have to take an interest in me or my family and didn't have to do a thing for us, yet he did. He is just that kind of man who would take an interest in young black men's lives and had the desire to help inspire people to keep pressing on to achieve their goals and dreams. He supervises a youth organization and organizes trips annually to tour HBCU campuses, go to NBA games, and visit museums. He's also organized tours of the White House for young black boys and girls in the City of Omaha, most of whom have rarely left their neighborhood.

On his HBCU tours, especially, the kids get to see that there are colleges full of black kids who look just like them, and they could aspire to grow beyond the borders of the city and their neighborhood. All they had to do was believe it could happen and work toward making that dream a reality.

Travis and I remain close. I admire him, and I still look up to him to this day. He still works in his job, and he's still active in the community, inspiring young people across the city to attend college and live their dreams. He's probably one of the most well-rounded men and fathers I've ever met, though he would be the first to tell you he wasn't a perfect man. Travis is tremendously successful as a mentor, community builder, and father and brings passion, energy, and dedication to each of those roles. He is a naturally mature person who is emotionally intelligent and considerate of others.

While Travis is a success story, some men will find it much more challenging to be successful at anything because of the poor choices they make, especially in how they sow their seed. If there is one thing I wish more black men would consider, it is being responsible for sowing their seed and becoming fathers at the right time, and not having children by multiple women at a very young age. This situation has the most considerable influence on the kind of life that young black men are able to build for themselves. Many of the problems that result from making poor choices in this one area will have a long-lasting impact on their ability to enjoy the life they would otherwise have if they didn't have multiple children often by multiple women that they must provide for financially. This dynamic is avoidable and often comes with devastating consequences that can be hard to overcome.

Questions for Discussion

1. What did you learn about emotions growing up? Do you think it is okay for men to cry?
2. Is it hard for you to show emotion as a grown man? Can you recall a time when showing how you really felt helped you or someone else?
3. What will you teach your children or the boys you mentor about showing emotion?

5

Value Your Seed

In the circle of men, I've met throughout my life, I've met great fathers who made the job look easy because they put in the work and had all the available resources to help them thrive as dads. These men were by no means perfect, but who is? What they were was dedicated, hard-working, and decent men who valued the role they played in the lives of their children and made it a priority to show up and be present for their children, regardless of the circumstances. Other than their own self-motivation, the one thing that most of them also shared is that they typically had a stable co-parenting relationship with the mother or mothers of their children. Sometimes, the mother was his wife, sometimes, his significant other, and sometimes, his ex. Regardless of the relationship, they genuinely sought to have good lines of communication regarding parental discussions. Conversely, I've known men whose relationship with their children suffered tremendously for one primary reason: their inability to be responsible for the seeds they sowed with the women they had in their lives in the past. This is my cautionary tale to black men who have children with multiple women they are not in relationships with. Whether there is just one unplanned child or multiple unplanned children, my hope is that young black men will take responsibility for protecting themselves and the women in their lives from becoming "accidental parents."

A young black man's failure to prevent an unplanned pregnancy continues to wreak havoc financially, emotionally, and mentally long after consummation. It's imperative that men protect themselves and the women they care for from that responsibility before they are ready for it. This must be a priority. The ideal situation for a man who wants to be able to father a child responsibly is to be married or in a long-term relationship with the child's mother - not an accidental liaison that results in lifelong ties and ramifications.

I'm not trying to demonize men who aren't in a relationship with the mother of their children - things happen, but, as a good friend used to always say, "once is an accident, twice is a plan." I've known far too many men who fathered multiple children by multiple women, and it had an enormously detrimental impact on the life they had planned for themselves, not just financially but in many other ways as well.

One example is Lamar. He was the younger brother of a girl I dated many years ago. Lamar was charismatic, tall, and handsome and was really a lady's man. He made the critical mistake of being somewhat reckless and impregnating several different women at once. To this day, I am not sure whether it was seven or eight. The sad running joke among the people who knew him is that they would ask how many kids he was up to now every time they saw him. Lamar didn't find it funny at all. In fact, he suffered quite a bit due to the burden of having to provide for so many unplanned children. He wasn't a person who had bad intentions; he just didn't realize that his poor choices and irresponsible actions had consequences.

It would have been nearly impossible for Lamar to provide for eight children even if he had a six-figure income (which he didn't). He worked inconsistently and was in and out of jail for not paying child support, which of course, meant that even if he was able to land a job, he would get fired for not being at work because he was in jail.

With eight kids, Lamar wasn't able to participate in all his children's lives the way he should, and he didn't have a good relationship with the mothers of his children. Lamar didn't prepare himself to provide for those kids. He was the kind of guy who had a big personality and all the charisma in the world to attract women but had no ability whatsoever to self-regulate or plan anything beyond today. As a result, he never took the responsibility of fathering children seriously and wasn't really responsible for the lives he created.

I lost touch with Lamar when I stopped dating his sister. I don't know if he got himself together or had a relationship with any of his children. I always hoped that somehow, he would turn his life around and change his ways, but nothing that Lamar ever did gave me any confidence that would happen. Lamar was probably the first of several other men I knew who were in similar circumstances.

When I moved to Houston, I found a great barber and would regularly visit for a cut. The barbershop for black men is a place where men, young and old, come together. One day, when I was at the barbershop, which was usually filled with older black men, I found mostly young men waiting. As I sat waiting to get my hair cut, one of the young men being cut by another barber was complaining, rather loudly, about a guy he was friends with who went to jail for not paying child support, and the guy was blaming the mother of the child. Several of the other young men were chiming in and agreeing with this sentiment.

All of a sudden, an older gentleman named J.D., who I knew to be a correctional officer in his late 50s, got really quiet, and you could tell he was listening intently. Now J.D. was a nice guy, but he didn't play games and wasn't about jokes. We were hearing the dudes talk, and he yelled out, "Man, forget him!" Except, J.D., the F word used by J.D., was not forget. J.D. went on to tell the young guys that the guy he was talking about was all wrong. "The only time you have control over the situation with a woman when you have children is when you decide to have children or not," J.D. told him. "All of you have seen situations when a dude got hemmed up with a kid, and he had no control over any of it. Whether she decides to keep the child, whether you got custody or visitation. The only time you have control is when you choose to protect yourself or not. So, a man who chooses not to protect himself has to be responsible for the position he put himself in."

He was absolutely right.

That lecture happened after I'd met the woman who would become my wife, but it happened during my twenties, when men are most likely to become fathers. J.D.'s words stuck with me that day, and I realized that he was absolutely right. Still, sadly, too many men, it seemed, never had a person like J.D. advise them that they have to be more responsible for protecting their futures by protecting themselves from becoming fathers before they are ready. Lamar didn't have someone to tell him that it would hamper his future.... but unfortunately, Lamar isn't the only man I know who has placed himself in this situation.

There was another friend, Corey, who I'd known for many years growing up because his family and my family were friendly. Corey went through a bad breakup with his girl one year, and he was heartbroken and depressed about the situation. As a result, he did what I see many men do and went through what many refer to as a "ho phase." In the months following Corey's breakup with his girl, he had sexual relationships with multiple women. Unfortunately for him, four of those women happened to become pregnant at the same time and delivered babies in the same year. Corey was stuck being the father to four children by four different women and paying child support for each.

Corey and Lamar were different because Corey put himself in a situation where he could at least provide for them financially so he would keep himself out of the perils of child support. Still, his life wasn't easy. If he ended a relationship, he had to reveal to his new love that he had four children by four different women, and all of the kids were around the same age. Of course, that's a huge red flag with any woman he wants to date seriously. He also had an adversarial relationship with some of his children's mothers, and because of this, he couldn't be the type of father he wanted to be. He doesn't see his children as often as he'd like. He has to deal with far more tension that he wants to and navigate situations carefully so he can maintain relationships with his children.

When I look at the situations Lamar and Corey put themselves in, I think J.D. said it best when he said the only control you have over the type of family you'll raise in the future starts with you and whether you choose to protect yourself or not. Because of the patriarchal system we live in, we place a lot of emphasis on telling young women to not sleep around. But the mistake we make is not giving that same lesson to our young men. They are held by a different standard and often praised by some men in our community for sleeping with multiple women. As a young man, I can remember that adults, both women and men, would ask me how many girlfriends I had, while my girl cousins could only have a boy come by and sit in the living room, and they had to be watched like a hawk at all times by her parents. This rarely happens to boys. Too often, they are encouraged to pursue multiple women. As a result, many boys grow up balancing several girls at one time and not taking precautions to prevent a pregnancy or sexually transmitted diseases.

We have to teach our young men to value their bodies and protect themselves. Often times a woman who may have had a high number of sexual encounters and how some people devalue her because of her promiscuity, we have to let it be known that that same judgment should be placed on young black men as well. Instead, the only "judgment" often comes when these men are ushered into court by the mother of their child or children and ordered to pay child support for those children.

The situation isn't always a complete failure, however. As I said, Corey is a good man who is a loving father who now wants to offer the best to his children. He is also in a different place with his maturity and isn't trying to have sex with as many women as possible. But finding a woman who won't judge him for his history with relationships and won't rule him out as a serious mate because of his limited ability to provide for her or additional children that they have is a serious constraint on developing a future relationship.

Too often, young black men are raised in single-parent households with a woman giving many life lessons and dispensing the wisdom they will need to safely reach adulthood from a woman's point of view. This doesn't mean that mothers can't instill in their sons the same values they would instill in their girls regarding being responsible for protecting themselves. Mothers often have a strong influence over this. They set the tone for the type of woman a young man looks for. She is often also invested in making sure that a young man knows how to make a wise decision regarding the type of woman you should date seriously. Most mothers want their sons' potential mates to have the characteristics that she possesses and will drill this into their young men regardless of whether he gets advice from his father or any other man that happens to be involved in his life.

Parents have an enormous ability to influence their young men's decisions regarding how to treat and date a woman and what characteristics are most important when thinking about your future. One of the primary duties we as parents have is to make sure that the values we hold are passed onto the next generation. This includes how to take responsibility and accountability for your health (including sexual health), how to maintain emotional, physical, and fiscal stability, and how to put yourself in the best position to have a bright future. I'm sure that most men who find themselves in the position of being young fathers don't recall having parents so strict that they couldn't be let out of their sight when dating a girl or being constantly lectured that they needed to protect themselves from sexually transmitted diseases or pregnancy the way that young women are. I would like to see that change.

It was J.D., who had no relationship to me or any other men in the barbershop, who took the time to put to bed the notion that a woman owes us something when it is our obligation as men to take care of the children we produce. He taught us that our futures - when it comes to children and women - is solely determined by us. He was right about that and the lesson stuck with me and it's one that I instilled not just in my own children but in any other child who becomes a part of my village. I say a village because it takes more than a mother and a father to raise a child in this day and age. To some, that old saying has lost its value. I believe we need to change that.

Questions for Discussion

1. What did you learn about sexuality growing up? Did you learn that it was okay for men to have sexual relationships with multiple women? What will you teach your sons or the young men you mentor about this?
2. If you have children, what is your relationship like with your children's mother? Whether married or not, what are you teaching your children about how their mother should be treated?
3. What advice would you give to a young boy who is just starting to develop romantic relationships? What advice would you give a young man who already has fathered children but is not yet mature enough to take care of them?

6

The Village

Each of the men I chose to highlight in this book taught me something about fatherhood and the importance of being present for your children. They impacted my journey as a father and were also a part of the community of individuals who made up my "village." In every sense of the word, the men who helped me become a supportive and engaged father didn't just impact my life but also the lives of my children. They became the tribe or group that the ancestors spoke about when they said, "it takes a village to raise a child."

We've all seen what happens when kids act out or deviate from what you've taught them all their lives about how to conduct themselves appropriately. Even in the earliest years of parenting, we are teaching our kids how to abide by rules, be respectful and take their educational opportunities seriously, but that doesn't always mean that their actions will align with what we taught them. The village is important because these are people who will feel absolutely no hesitation to correct or redirect your child in your absence and even in your presence. They are folks your child knows and respects, and more importantly, they are people who have beliefs and values that align with yours and who help reinforce the lessons and values you've instilled in your children.

Black children are confronted with a range of problems in society that, in many instances, make surviving their most formidable challenge. While the men I talked about within these pages were exemplary fathers who were present and engaged in their children's lives, many black children, unfortunately, do not have that example. This is when having a village is all the more important, though sadly, we don't see that nearly as much as we should in the Black community. There's a hesitance for many Black men to stand in the gap where a father is not present. But we need men to step up to be a part of the village to ensure that our children are in the best position to not only survive but thrive as adults. We need a network of people looking out for our children. As a father and a Black man who has strived to remain active and involved in the community, I have seen this firsthand.

The community of fathers and surrogate fathers that make up my immediate network all have the same general standards and beliefs in hard work, integrity, education, self-respect, and honor. These men also feel a sense of responsibility to give back to the communities they are a part of through their volunteer work as coaches, mentors, and surrogate fathers. Occasionally, they were told that they were the only male role models that some kids had to look up to, which made the mission to nurture and encourage the young people they interacted with even more critical.

In most cases, sports were a unifying activity among my community – a common hobby that we could engage in that offered positive benefits to the dads and kids involved. It kept us active and provided an outlet for the stressors that everyone encounters. Sports continue to give young people, especially young boys, a way to occupy their free time that is constructive and includes one-on-one time with positive male figures who are willing to listen and encourage. Most of the men in my network were good examples of positive male role models. Some routinely mentored children that were not family members. Others served as father figures to children outside of their nuclear families but related to the extended family. In some cases, these men had to step up when the birth parents or nuclear family members had neither the means nor the motivation to invest in the children's lives. In others, they simply served the purpose of reinforcing the lessons that were instilled by involved parents. That is my role with my Godson, Christopher.

Christopher's household had two involved parents, but I served as that alternative voice to reinforce their guidance whenever needed. I would do this not just for Christopher, but for other young men that I met through the various athletic teams and community activities that my network was engaged in. These were young men who I consistently gave words of advice, motivation, love, and encouragement. That is something that to this day, I feel comfortable doing. I'm also confident that it helped keep these young men on the right path in life.

One of the most critical roles of the village is men stepping up when a father figure isn't available to do so. When our children, especially our young men, encounter some of their most challenging years, from 12 to 18, they need the guidance of a father figure for advice, motivation, encouragement, and love, and they need it consistently. It's not enough to show up occasionally and applaud them for excelling in sports, but you also need to check in on them to see how they're doing with their studies, what they're interested in, and how they spend their free time. Keeping them out of trouble and inspiring them to do their best requires that you know more about them than their favorite sport or what girl they have a crush on. Young men need consistent, positive influences in their lives as well as someone to remind them of the cautionary stories I've shared in this book regarding what can happen when men fail to plan for children and wind up becoming a parent because they didn't take their own futures into consideration when they needed to.

As I noted, one of the many ways that men can influence young lives is being a father figure in the lives of young men in their extended families. I'm glad to know that there are men like my best friend, Bruce, who can stand in the gap when young men don't have that fatherly voice and encouragement.

Bruce had several nieces and nephews in his family, but his relationship with his nephew, Marcus, was a tight bond. Marcus was the product of two teen parents. It's no secret that very young parents can't possibly be as prepared for all that parenthood demands, even if they have family support, and that was the case with Marcus.

From the very beginning, Marcus' father was not in the picture in any meaningful way. Marcus always knew who his father was but rarely saw him or spoke to him. Marcus did, however, have strong women in his life. Though these women were a constant presence that he could rely on as a child, he lacked a male role model, so Bruce stepped in.

Even though Marcus and Bruce lived in different cities, I witnessed firsthand the lengths that Bruce would go through to support his nephew when he needed it the most. It seemed to me as if Bruce promised himself that Marcus would know what it was like to have a man show up for him and remain involved in his life simply because he knew that Marcus needed that male interaction and support. It was a beautiful thing to witness. Bruce couldn't drive to be present for Marcus; he had to fly to attend those events. Whether it was band recitals or elementary, middle, or high school graduation ceremonies, Bruce was there. Bruce was present for holidays and consistently called Marcus to check in on him, offering encouragement or correction as needed. There was also the occasional pop-up visit when Marcus would get off track, and forceful redirection was warranted and needed. Bruce had no qualms about spending his time and money to see that Marcus had the father figure he needed but didn't really have.

While Bruce had the resources and determination to do this, even long-distance, this type of involvement is rare and speaks volumes about Bruce's character and commitment. More importantly, it made a huge difference in the life of his nephew, who is now grown and successful.

James, who we talked about earlier, had younger cousins who needed a male influence and also served that role. Sparky was a father figure for countless young men he taught in the classroom and coached on the football field. Travis served as a role model for all of the young children he guided in North Omaha and enlisted several other men that served in that role for the children he couldn't reach on a one-to-one basis. My Dad, Marvin Senior, also served as a surrogate father for all of his family, not just my brothers and me.

People often think that it requires being bonded by blood to be committed enough or caring enough to invest in young men's' lives when all it really takes is the willingness to remain consistent, establish a bond, and demonstrate that you are living the values that you're attempting to instill in the lives of the young men you seek to encourage. It doesn't mean you have to be perfect either. Some of the men that were part of my village had challenges with relationships of their own at times, but they never shied away from the responsibility of being present for the young men they sought to impact. Often, it just took a little encouragement or a simple phone call, which everyone can do, to make a difference.

The best part is that the men that grow up having that influence and bond that came from establishing a solid relationship with a man of the village is that they in turn pay that investment forward, choosing to commit themselves to having an impact on the lives of the next generation of young men. Most often, this didn't require a huge financial commitment but a significant investment of time, either in person or by telephone, to make a difference to the child. That example of commitment and compassionate service pays dividends as young boys mature into men, and it sets the example for a life of involvement, leadership, and community service. That is the kind of engagement that has the potential to build up our communities to reach even the most challenging achievements.

Questions for Discussion

1. Was there someone in your life who encouraged you and inspired you as you grew up? Who was in your village?
2. Are there young men around you who you can inspire and encourage?
3. What special gift, talent, or ability can you share with the next generation?

7

Evolving as a Father

The first step to becoming an involved father is just to be present. Without making excuses for those men who choose not to be, as a black man, it can be tough to be there for your children as much as you'd like to be - especially if you have experienced some setbacks in life. Whether it's work, financial challenges, relationship struggles with their mother, or just competing demands for your time, prioritizing the young people in your life can be trying. Still, my experience has been that you will regret not making your role as a father your top priority. The future of your children is at stake and your role in shaping them is invaluable.

It is my desire and hope that the lessons and knowledge that I gained from the men I talk about in this book will cause you to think about the men in your life who have served as those role models for fatherhood. While you may not have men who stand out as ideal fathers, I'm sure that there are men you know and see on a regular basis who show up and are very active in the lives of their children - even when they still have work to do on themselves. There's a certain type of man who recognizes that although he has personal milestones to reach, his presence is essential in his children's lives. Your kids don't expect you to be perfect, and you shouldn't wait for all the stars to align in your life to be there for your kids. All they really want is your time.

I hope you will refer to this book to remind you of the lessons that can be learned when men lead by example. The men I profiled in this book offered lessons on being present, loving, and supportive. It's important to note that none of the men I mentioned in this book were perfect individuals - in fact, if I were to talk about them in totality, you'd see that they were far from it - but they are good men and good fathers. I've shown my frailties and imperfections (and theirs) because I like to learn from mistakes. Even though the men I talked about weren't perfect, they still chose to be active and to participate to be a positive influence in the lives of the children they cared about. You don't have to have the perfect body, the right words, or an ivy league education…. you just have to participate and do. You have to give your best at all times.

It is said that a smart man learns from his mistakes, and a wise man learns from others' mistakes. I want you to be a wise man. You should know that the life lessons that I talk about in this book won't be applicable all at one time. The struggles, the problems, and the obstacles that I faced as a new father in his 20s are much different than the problems I had as a middle-aged man with young adults. At various periods in your life, you may have to refer to this book for some insights and wisdom that will guide you as you work to develop bonds with your children that will cement the foundation of your relationship for a lifetime. That doesn't mean that there won't be challenges that make growth and progress difficult during some periods of your child's life. I'm sure that fathers who are currently raising teenagers can relate when I say that the most challenging years are those between 12 and

16, when your kids will test your patience, their boundaries, your tolerance, and your commitment. As they challenge you, remember that they're also navigating uncharted territory and teenage emotions and will do and say things that are contradictory to everything that you've taught them. As you recall the examples and the lessons from the men in this book, which I hope you will refer to often, remember the guidance and lessons that will help you make it through to the other side of those years while maintaining a strong bond with your child.

My final word of advice: whether you know it or not, young men, especially young fathers, are watching you speak, act, and react to the challenge of fatherhood, and they are learning from your example. They may never acknowledge it, but they are storing in their memory bank the things they witness you say and do, and they will use that in the future with their own kids—mark my words. Give them the truth. Unadulterated and real. But also make sure that they know they don't have to be perfect. They just have to start with being present.

Questions for Discussion

1. Which of the men profiled did you identify with most? What did you see in that character that was inspirational or cautionary?
2. What have you learned in this book that could help you as a father, future father, father-figure, or mentor?
3. Are there any young men in your life who you could start being a role model to? Who is a part of your village or whose village could you be a part of?

www.ingramcontent.com/pod-product-compliance
Lightning Source LLC
Chambersburg PA
CBHW062157100526
44589CB00014B/1859